STAND UP AND SPEAK OUT

Strike Now!

*The Pilauski Family During
the Coal Miners' Strike of 1902*

By Gare Thompson
Illustrated by Marcy Ramsey

Produced through the worldwide resources of
the National Geographic Society, John M.
Fahey, Jr., President and Chief Executive
Officer; Gilbert M. Grosvenor, Chairman of the
Board; Nina D. Hoffman, Executive Vice
President and President, Books and Education
Publishing Group.

**Prepared by National Geographic School
Publishing**
Ericka Markman, Senior Vice President and
President, Children's Books and Education
Publishing Group; Steve Mico, Senior Vice
President, Publisher, Editorial Director; Francis
Downey, Executive Editor; Richard Easby,
Editorial Manager; Bea Jackson, Director of
Design; Cindy Olson, Art Director; Margaret
Sidlosky, Director of Illustrations; Matt
Wascavage, Manager of Publishing Services;
Lisa Pergolizzi, Sean Philpotts, Production
Managers, Ted Tucker, Production Specialist.

Manufacturing and Quality Control
Christopher A. Liedel, Chief Financial Officer;
Phillip L. Schlosser, Director; Clifton M.
Brown, Manager.

Editors
Barbara Seeber, Mary Anne Wengel

Book Development
Morrison BookWorks LLC

Book Design
Steven Curtis Design

Art Direction
Dan Banks, Project Design Company

Map Development and Production
Mapping Specialists, Ltd.

Published by the National Geographic Society
1145 17th Street, N.W.
Washington, D.C. 20036-4688

ISBN: 978-0-7922-5868-1
ISBN: 0-7922-5868-1

3 4 5 6 7 8 9 10 11 20 19 18 17 16 15 14
Printed in the U.S.A.

✑ Contents ✑

America and Coal

Coal is a black substance that can be burned to provide heat. It is often found deep underground. Coal has played an important part in America's history. During the 19th century, an industrial revolution took place. At this time, many new industries were developed. Factories were built to make things for people to use. Machines in the factories could do work faster than ever before. The machines were powered by steam. The steam was made by heating water. The water was heated by burning coal. New steam engines were used to power trains and ships. People also burned coal to heat their homes. By 1900, coal was the main source of power in the United States. Without coal, the country would have ground to a halt.

Before the Anthracite Strike of 1902

1701
Coal is discovered in the United States.

1700   1720   1740

These boys worked in the coal mines in the early 1900s.

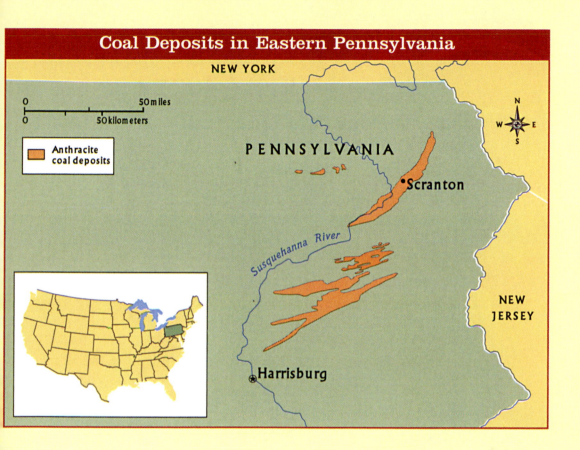

Coal Deposits in Eastern Pennsylvania

NEW YORK

PENNSYLVANIA

Susquehanna River

•Scranton

NEW JERSEY

⊛Harrisburg

0 ⊢ 50 miles
0 ⊢ 50 kilometers

Anthracite coal deposits

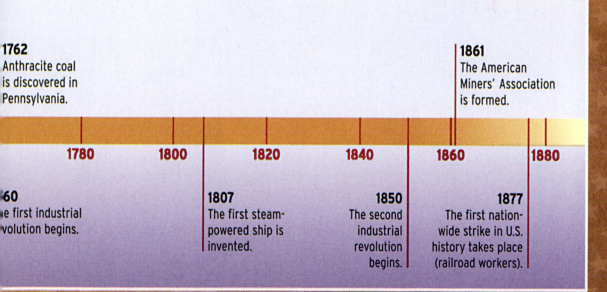

1762
Anthracite coal is discovered in Pennsylvania.

1861
The American Miners' Association is formed.

1780 1800 1820 1840 1860 1880

60
e first industrial volution begins.

1807
The first steam-powered ship is invented.

1850
The second industrial revolution begins.

1877
The first nation-wide strike in U.S. history takes place (railroad workers).

The Characters

The Pilauski Family

Thomas

Thomas, the oldest son, is 16 years old. He is a smart boy who is learning to read. He works in the mines with his father, but yearns for a life outside the mines. Thomas believes the miners should strike.

Dorothy

Dorothy, the middle child, is 13 years old. After school and on Saturdays, she works as a clerk at the company store. Dorothy is a dreamer and immerses herself in books.

Irene

Irene, the mother, is 36 years old, but she looks years older. She works hard to care for her family, but has found time to learn to read. She reads with her children whenever she can.

Stanley

Stanley, the father, is 37 years old. He has worked in the mines since he was 16. The labor and dust in the mines have worn him down, but he is loyal to his employer.

Other Characters

Narrator
Miner
Union Leader
Mother Jones
Reporter
Soldier
Striking miner
Elevator man
Stable hand
Workers 1-4

Peter

Peter, the youngest child, is 8 years old. He loves the idea of working in the mines because he admires his father and older brother.

 Act I

The Setting

Scranton, Pennsylvania, 1902

Scene 1

The Pilauski home in early evening

Narrator: Imagine a small town in Pennsylvania a hundred years ago. The streets are lined with small row houses. Everywhere there is coal dust—on the pavement, on the windowsills, on the few sickly trees. On the hillsides in the distance are the towering wooden structures where the miners work every day. These structures house mining equipment, tools, and **breakers,** machines that are used to break up the coal coming out of the mine. Pouring from these buildings are miners just finishing their long shifts. They trudge silently home, carrying lunch pails, their faces and clothes black with the dust and dirt of the mines.

Suddenly, a loud whistle starts to blow, sounding the alarm that there has been an accident or a death in the mines. Soon, at the top of a hill, a mule-drawn cart

---

breaker – a machine used to break up rocks or coal

comes into view. As the cart rattles along, people come to their doors and windows to stare and to follow its progress down the street. They all know the cart. They call it the Black Maria. It serves as both an ambulance and a hearse. Another miner, badly injured or dead, is being carried home to his family.

Dorothy: *(Looking out the window)* Mother! Come quick! The Black Maria is turning down our street.

Irene: Look! It's gone past the Smith family's house. It's coming toward us! There's Peter with a bunch of boys running alongside the cart.

Dorothy: What is Peter doing? Is he trying to signal to us?

Irene: Oh, thank heavens. It's going past.

(Peter runs across the street and to his house.)

Peter: *(Out of breath)* Ma, Dorothy, don't worry. It's just old Mr. Dugowitz.

Irene: Peter Pilauski! No son of mine will show disrespect for another miner. Do you hear me?

Peter: Yes, Ma. Sorry. I didn't mean no disrespect. I'm just happy it's not Pa or Thomas.

Irene: I know, son, but Mr. Dugowitz was a fine man. He taught your father about mining when we first moved here. He was always kind and generous to us.

(Dorothy and Irene watch from the window.)

Dorothy: Ma! There's Pa and Thomas coming down the street.

(The Black Maria stops in front of the Dugowitz's house. The cart drivers carry the body of Mr. Dugowitz inside.)

Dorothy: People will be starting to gather at their house. Someone should get Father John from the church.

Irene: Dorothy, you go after Father John, while I will get supper on the table. We will pay our respects to the Dugowitzes after we eat.

Dorothy: OK, Ma, I'll go. I'll be back in a few minutes.

(Dorothy exits. She enters a few moments later with Stanley and Thomas.)

Irene: Stanley, Thomas, I'm so glad you're home. Dorothy, did you find Father John?

Dorothy: Yes, Ma, he's on his way.

Irene: Dorothy, we should bake tonight. We'll prepare some bread and meat pies for the family. I don't know what will become of poor Mrs. Dugowitz.

Stanley: She'll get her husband's pay for the month. Then she'll move in with her son. Maybe we can help build a small room for her—if the company lets us.

Dorothy: She has to leave her home? That's not right, Pa.

Stanley: The company owns the house. The widow only rents it. As long as her husband worked in the mine, she could stay there. But now she has to move out. Those are the rules.

Thomas: That's why we need a strong union, to protect us all against things like that. A union will represent the miners.

Stanley: Well, we'll have to see, Thomas. Peter, what did you do in school today?

Peter: Nothing much, Pa. You know I'm eight now. There's nothing more for me to learn. I'm the same age as Thomas when he started in the mines as a breaker boy.

Stanley: You are not going down into the mines. At least not yet. You must stay in school and learn to read and write.

Peter: Pa, we need the money. If I were a breaker boy, I could earn enough to buy bread and some meat, too. I could even give some to the widow.

Stanley: Peter, that's a nice idea. But do you know what breaker boys do?

Peter: Yes, I think so.

Stanley: I don't think you do. They sit on hard benches and straddle long **troughs** of coal moving underneath them. The machines shake the whole place. The breaker boys can't talk to anybody because there is so much dust and noise. Their hands get black and bloody. And the money they make in a whole day won't buy a loaf of bread. For Thomas and I, working in the mines is honest work. It's a good job, and we live all right. We're better off than my father was in Poland. He

---

trough – a long, shallow, often V-shaped channel along which coal is moved from one place to another

worked himself to death and never even owned the land he worked. But Peter, if you stay in school, you could get a job that pays much better. One that's not nearly as hard on your body.

Thomas: We don't own this house, Peter. It belongs to Mr. Van Buten. He owns the mine, and he owns the company store. He owns everything. If you get a good education, you could own your own land and your own house someday.

Dorothy: Ma and I have heard the miners talk at the store. They say that the union will protect the miners, and soon you'll get better wages. Well, that is, if you decide to strike.

Stanley: Be careful what you say, Dorothy. I'm not so sure the union is doing the right thing by planning a strike. Right now, we get free medical care. We can visit the doctor when we want and never have to pay.

Thomas: Sure, that's because the doctor can't do anything for us except tell us our lungs are black and we're gonna die. I bet that's what happened to poor Mr. Dugowitz—his lungs just gave out.

Irene: Thomas Pilauski, you hush. Your father has worked hard all his life to provide for us. I won't have you making comments that are insulting to him and his job. Now, finish your meal.

Thomas: Yes, ma'm. I didn't mean nothing against you, Pa.

Stanley: I know, son. It's hard to see things like this happen to a fellow miner. Let's stop talking about the mines. We spend enough time down inside 'em.

Dorothy: I'm reading a book about slaves in the South. It's called *Uncle Tom's Cabin*. I can read some of that to you. It's real good—and real sad.

Thomas: Good thing I don't keep a diary. Now *that* would make you cry.

Stanley: Yes, maybe after we pay our respects to the Dugowitzes, you could read to us, Dorothy. Your stories always help take our minds off things. I sure do like to hear you read.

Dorothy: Sure, Pa. *(Pausing)* The teacher says that she needs an assistant. The mines will pay for the assistant for next year 'cause there are so many kids now. She thinks I should apply for the job. I'm almost 14 and there's not much else that she can teach me. So, what do you think?

Irene: *(Clearing the table)* Oh, my, imagine our daughter teaching! You will make us so proud, Dorothy.

Thomas: That sounds great, Dorothy. You'd make a very good teacher.

Stanley: Well, let's make our visit to the widow. Most of the other miners and their families will probably be there by now. Hopefully we can give her some comfort. It is a sad duty, but I want to tell her what a good man her husband was.

Scene 2

Sunday evening in the Pilauski home

Narrator: After the funeral, the miners and their families gathered at the widow Dugowitz's house. The women helped her pack her things, and the men sipped coffee and talked about what a good miner Mr. Dugowitz was. A fiddler played the Russian songs that were his favorites. The miners and their wives sang and talked until the sun set and then returned to their homes in the neighborhood.

Stanley: You know, Mr. Dugowitz worked in the mines for over 30 years. He started as a breaker boy, just like Thomas did.

Thomas: Yes and he ended up a breaker boy. His bad lungs wouldn't allow him to work underground. They found him slumped over the trough. Mr. Dugowitz was only 40 years old. I don't want to end up like that.

Irene: Thomas, don't talk like that. Eat your dinner; you need your strength. You, too, Peter.

Peter: I'm not hungry.

Irene: Be glad that there is food on the table, Peter.

Peter: I still say if you'd let me go to work, then we'd eat better.

Stanley: Enough, Peter. You are not working in the mines and that's final. I want you to work hard at school so maybe you won't have to be a miner.

Thomas: So, Pa, what do you think about the talk of a strike?

Stanley: Well, I'm not sure. The last time there was a strike, we got a little more money, but we didn't get paid while we were on strike, so we fell into more debt. And who knows what the owners will do? Might fire us all. More people are moving to Pennsylvania every day. And they'll work for next to nothing. Won't bother them that we are on strike.

Thomas: But if we don't strike Pa, it's like the owners own us.

Stanley: They don't own us, Thomas. We're not slaves like in that *Uncle Tom's Cabin* story that Dorothy read to us. She's a fine reader, that girl. She's so smart.

Thomas: So am I, Pa. Dorothy has been very good about teaching me to read and write. I can't read as well as she can, but I can read. I read what the union leaders write. They say we should get more money and shorter hours. That makes sense to me.

Stanley: Maybe the strike is a good idea, but it worries me. I just don't know, Thomas.

Thomas: Well, I do. I'm going to support the strike. You don't want the other miners to be mad at you, Pa. You have to vote for it. There is no other way.

Scene 3

In the mines

Narrator: It is midafternoon on a workday when a deafening noise and the sound of rushing water fill the mine. A tunnel has caved in from water pressure. The whistle blows, signaling an accident. Fearful that Thomas is trapped under a pile of rocks, Stanley rushes to the scene. He crawls along the collapsed tunnel to the point where the tunnel is blocked by a pile of rocks. Dust from the **rubble** hits him full in the face as he crawls. It takes him only a few minutes, though it seems like hours as he wonders what he will find. Stanley joins other men as they work to free the men on the other side. The men work in teams to remove the rock that separates them from the injured miners. They can hear men moaning from the other side, and they can also hear water rushing into the tunnel.

---

rubble – broken fragments of rock

Stanley: *(Shouting)* Do you know who was over there? I think it might be where my son was working.

Worker 1: Don't know. But this is just another reason why we need a union to make this mine a safer place.

Stanley: Start pulling rocks out. But be careful; we don't want the roof falling on us. Anyone know how many men are in there?

Miner: There's a team of about ten. Let's get one of the mule boys in here. The mules can carry the rocks out.

Stanley: Form a line. The top part here looks safe. Make holes over that side so the water will seep out. Come on, men, move it! Could be your brother or son on the other side!

Worker 2: OK, I can see light through there now.

Worker 3: Now I can see them. Looks like two of them could have broken legs. And another one is bad.

Worker 4: Oh, here's the mule boy. Good work. Hard to get that mule in this small space.

Thomas: Midnight is a good mule. He does what I say. We're a team.

Worker 4: OK, men, let's get these men into the cart.

Stanley: *(Hugging Thomas)* Thank goodness you are all right, Thomas. I was so worried.

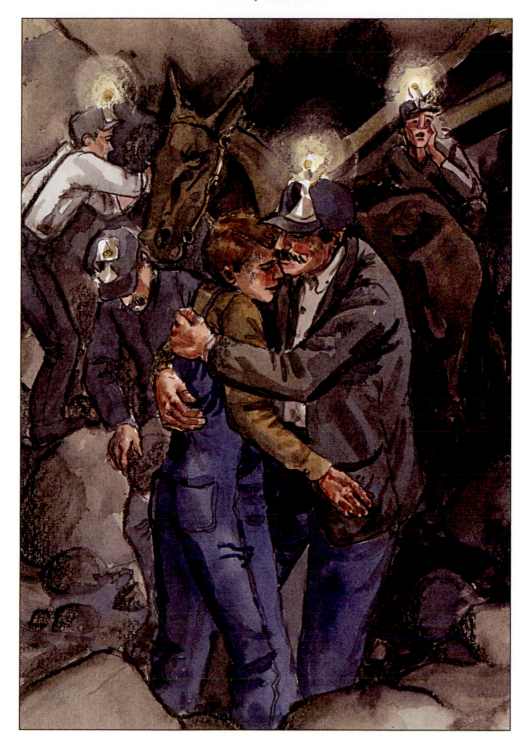

Thomas: I was worried it was you, Pa. How are the men who were trapped?

Stanley: Broken bones, mostly, but those can mend. Rocks crushed Walter Czub, though. He might have a broken back.

Thomas: Pa, if he does, it's over for him. He won't be able to bend over to mine. Pa, he's got four young kids.

Stanley: We'll look out for him, Thomas. We have to stick together.

Worker 1: OK, we've got everyone in the cart now. We should get moving. It's too dangerous down here.

Thomas: It feels like a furnace in here. Midnight looks like he's about to collapse. Don't worry, fella, we'll be moving in a minute.

Stanley: I've been thinking more about a strike. The mine owners are not going to improve things unless we demand it.

Thomas: I think that's true, Pa. I'm glad you've changed your mind.

Stanley: I don't like making demands, but I don't see any other way.

Thomas: You're right, Pa. Maybe we can get the union president to come to this mine. He would get all the miners behind a strike. Things have gotten pretty bad here. We couldn't lose.

Stanley: Good idea. But now you need to get going with these injured men. The tunnel could collapse any minute.

Thomas: Pa, you come with me. We both better get out of here.

 Act II

The Setting

Scranton, Pennsylvania, 1902

Scene 1

At a miners' meeting, May 1902

Narrator: The miners and some of their families have gathered for a meeting at the union headquarters. The union members want to go on strike. While the majority of miners are in favor of the strike, there are a few miners who oppose it. Immigrants are pouring into the United States in large numbers, and many miners fear that the mine owners will hire these new immigrants to replace them, as they have in the past.

As the Pilauski family enters the meeting and finds their seats, the air is tense. Going on strike is risky for the miners. The mine owners hold the deeds to their homes, pay their medical costs, and cover the schooling costs for their children. Also, some fear that the mine owners will raise prices at the company store, where the miners buy all their food and clothes on credit. A speaker from the union stands up to talk to the miners.

Union Leader: Tonight is a great occasion. Here in Scranton we have as our guest, a great human being. Her name is Mary Harris Jones, but most of you know her as Mother. She has worked hard for unions and workers for the last 20 years. She has led marches and protests. She knows what is right. Fellow miners, I give you the miners' angel, Mother Jones.

Mother Jones: *(Walking briskly to the front of the meeting hall)* First of all, let me tell you, I'm not a do-gooder; I'm a fire-starter. And I've come here tonight to tell you why you in Scranton must seize the moment. I've come to tell you why you must strike.

The first reason is for yourselves and your families. You don't earn enough money to support your families. You work too many hours each day in terrible conditions.

The second reason is for your fellow workers. America has changed. It's gone from an agricultural to an industrial nation—and you must stand up with millions of your fellow workers and form strong unions. Unions will represent the workers of the United States. They will fight for better pay and better working conditions for everyone.

The third reason is because you are an arrow to the future. You must pave the way to better lives for those who come after you. Unions must be recognized so that workers can be protected now and in the coming years. You must stand up and speak out for what you believe in. Even when the battle seems hopeless, you must fight for your rights.

(Miners stand and cheer.)

Union Leader: Well, men, now it is time to choose. So what do you say? Should we strike or not? Let's take a vote.

Miners: Yes! Let's strike!

Narrator: The miners vote, and almost every hand goes up in favor of a strike. Even those who do not speak English are raising their hands to strike. But as the crowd quiets down and the reality of a strike hits, some begin to question the action.

Miner: How do we live during the strike? I don't have any savings. Everything I need I have to buy at the company store. The mine owner can call in my bill. How will I pay for everything? Who's going to feed my children? Who's going to put clothes on their backs? They have nothing to do with this and I won't let them suffer for it. Our families count on us to provide for them. We can't let them down.

Union Leader: The union will support you during the strike. You won't have to let your families down. You heard Mother Jones; now is the time. The country needs coal—they need us, so we'll have the upper hand.

Stanley: If we go on strike, we need to say what we want. I know we're all tired of worrying if we are going to make it out of the mine alive every day. And tired of worrying what will happen to our families if we don't. But what other reasons will we give for going on strike? There are many ways our jobs could be improved. We have to tell them what we want and we can't back down.

Union Leader: Mr. Pilauski is right. We need to make the message clear: More money! Shorter days! Better conditions! A tunnel collapses at least once a month. How many men here have been trapped in a shaft? And look at the young ones. Now they can stand up straight, and their lungs are fine, but what will they be like in ten years? Their backs will be bent, and their lungs will be filled with coal dust. We have to improve our working conditions.

(The men begin muttering and agreeing with what is being said.)

Miner: What if the owners hire others to do our work? Then we lose our jobs and our homes. New people are coming here every day. They want our jobs.

Union Leader: That won't happen. The strike will be swift and short. The owners will have to deal with us.

(The meeting breaks up and the Pilauski family walks home.)

Dorothy: Oh, Pa, thanks for bringing us. Mother Jones was wonderful. She made the miners so hopeful. I loved what she said about fighting even when the battle seems hopeless.

Thomas: So did I, Dorothy. And what she said makes sense. Why should the mine owners get rich on our hard labor? Without us, they'd have nothing. They should be more willing to share the wealth.

Stanley: Ah, Thomas, you sound dangerous now.

Thomas: No, Pa, I sound like a union member.

Scene 2

Outside the mine, September 1902

Narrator: The strike has been going on for more than three months. Newspapers report on it daily. Now that it is fall, the American people are beginning to worry. What if the miners are on strike during winter?

Will there be enough coal to heat their homes? The costs of fuel are beginning to rise. People want action because they feel that the strike has been going on for too long. As the scene opens, a reporter is interviewing Stanley and Thomas.

Reporter: So what do you hope to gain by this strike?

Stanley: We want decent wages, shorter hours, and safer conditions. And we want our union to be recognized. We need to be able to bargain with the mine owners.

Thomas: I earn less than a dollar a day. My ears ring from the noise of the coal rumbling up and down the breaker. Now that we're on strike, you hear only the noise of the marchers as they protest. It's never this quiet when the mines are open.

Reporter: What about all the American families that will be without heat this winter? What do you say to them? Do you want people to freeze to death? Do you think it's fair that they should suffer when they have had nothing to do with this strike?

Stanley: No, of course not. But we have to stand up for ourselves. Why should the mine owners get rich while we have nothing? Have you ever been down in a mine? You'd be on our side if you had. We're sorry for families who will be without coal this winter. But our lives are in danger each day we work in the mine.

Reporter: Everybody has to earn a living. What makes you so different?

Stanley: I want to earn a living as much as anyone. Do you think you could work hunched over for hours at a time? Most miners can't even stand up in the shafts. Water seeps in and tunnels cave in. We barely make enough money to feed our families. We want better pay and working conditions, and we deserve them.

Reporter: Sounds like an awful lot of complaining to me.

Stanley: You asked for my side of the story, and I gave it to you. Every word of it is true. But I suppose you will just write what you want to write. You reporters never take the side of the workingman.

Thomas: Well, Pa, I think it's time for us to go home. This reporter obviously doesn't see our side of things. And I'm getting hungry.

Stanley: *(As they walk home)* You know, son, I'm starting to get worried. It seems that no one understands our struggle. And paying the rent each month is getting pretty tough. The money I saved is gone. I want the strike to be over.

Thomas: I think it will be over soon. But in the meantime, we have to stand our ground.

Stanley: *(Later, at home)* So, Irene, you might read about me and Thomas on the front page of the newspaper tomorrow.

Irene: What did you do? Nothing bad, I hope.

Thomas: No, Pa just gave another one of his speeches. I think he should go into politics.

Dorothy: I'll look for it in the newspaper and read it to you all.

Thomas: Well, I've been reading the paper for myself. The strike has given me time to practice my reading. I've also read several of the books Dorothy's teacher gave her. They were really good. But I'm beginning to think that I'd rather be working.

Peter: Boy, I wish I were on strike. Who needs school?

Stanley: *You* do, Peter. You need school far more than you know. You and your sister have a chance to get out of this town, and I believe you will. *(Turns and looks at Thomas)* And I believe you will, too, Thomas, even though you started in the mines. You'll just have to fight a bit harder to do it.

Thomas: Once the strike is over, and we have the union to bargain for us, our lives are going to change. I know that things are going to be better with the union on our side.

Stanley: I hope so. The strike has to end soon. Let's eat while we still have food on the table.

Scene 3

At the Pilauski home, October 1902

Narrator: The strike has been going on now for more than a hundred days. The miners, who thought the strike would last less than a month, are worried. Some of them cannot pay what they owe at the company store. The union helps them a little, but some of the miners have begun to move out of the Scranton area to find work in other mines. As the scene opens, the family is sitting down to dinner. Things are tense—and the end of the strike is not in sight.

Stanley: The soup is good, Irene. But we don't need biscuits with every meal. Unfortunately, we're going to have to tighten our belts a little more. I don't know how much longer we're going to be able to get credit at the store. With no income, I don't know what we'll do if our credit runs out.

Thomas: We can't get discouraged, Pa. We need to stay strong. We knew it wasn't going to be easy.

Stanley: It's hard to stay strong when there's no food in your stomach, Thomas.

Dorothy: Yes, and if the strike does not end, then I will not be able to get a job as a teacher. There's even talk of closing the school. My teacher has given me some of her books to read while I'm home. They keep my mind off the things we don't have. I wish we could just end this strike.

Thomas: What we really need to do is stand our ground. The owners have to learn that they need us to keep the mine going. What do they have if they don't have workers? If we don't give in, it's bound to end soon.

Stanley: Yes, I think you're right, Thomas. The strike has to end soon. I've heard that President Roosevelt wants the strike to end. The governor of Pennsylvania is sending in soldiers to keep things orderly and safe. But some of the miners are getting rowdy, and I'm worried that there will be violence. Thomas, I want you to stay away from the rowdy crowd. We are not going to destroy the mine. We can't get involved in things like that.

Thomas: I wouldn't destroy anything, Pa. It's just that we need to make more noise when we march. You can't protest quietly if you want a response. The reporters love it, you know. People marching around in a group with their fists in the air—it makes a great picture for their newspapers.

Peter: It sounds like so much fun. Can I come with you?

Irene: No, Peter, you just heard your Pa and Thomas talking about all the violence there! You're too young to get involved in all of this. Stay home with me. I need your help here.

Peter: Oh, I'll stay out of trouble. I won't get in anybody's way. Please? Please, Pa?

Stanley: Well, Irene, the boy should see things the way they are. I'll keep him safe. *(Turning to Peter)* You can come by just once, Peter. You can miss school for a day. But only one day, and then it's back to school. Now, Dorothy, what are you going to read to us tonight? Nothing sad, I hope.

Dorothy: No, Pa. I have a play to read. It's about a prince who goes mad.

Thomas: He must have worked in the mines.

Dorothy: No. He was called Hamlet and he lived in Denmark a long time ago. A famous writer named Shakespeare wrote the story.

Stanley: Let Dorothy read. Her stories take my mind off of things and make it easier to sleep.

Thomas: Sorry. Go ahead Dorothy, tell us about your prince. I wonder what *he* had to deal with.

(Dorothy reads the first Act of Hamlet.*)*

Stanley: You're a wonderful reader, Dorothy, and that story is a good one so far. I'm looking forward to hearing some more of it tomorrow night. But now you and Peter must help your ma clean up. Thomas, let's step outside. *(Thomas and Stanley step out of the house.)* Here, look at this bill. It's for food. I can pay it this month, but I don't know what I'll do next month.

Thomas: Maybe I should go find work someplace else, Pa. I could try Philadelphia. There must be jobs there. I could also look for work in other coal mines. Maybe a job on the surface or in an office.

Stanley: But what would you do? You can't drive a mule in an office.

Thomas: No, but Dorothy has taught me to read, and I can write pretty well now. I bet I could write some pretty good stuff about what's happening. And I can add numbers now, too, Pa. I bet there are plenty of jobs for men who can do arithmetic.

Stanley: Well, let's think on it. It's time for bed. Got to save our voices for protesting on the **picket line.**

---

picket line — a group of people protesting at a workplace

Act III

The Setting

Scranton, Pennsylvania, October and November 1902

Scene 1

At the entrance to the gates of the mine

Narrator: The strike continues. Violence has broken out between miners and store owners and between miners who joined the strike and those who did not strike. Newspaper stories paint a picture of stubborn mine owners who refuse to give in to the demands of the miners. President Theodore Roosevelt has been asked to step in and end the strike, but he wants both sides to negotiate, or come to an agreement. He has invited both the mine owners and the union leaders to meet with him. As the act opens, there is a confrontation between the miners on strike, the working miners, and the military troops sent to protect the working miners. Stanley and Thomas look up to see Irene and Dorothy leading a group of women marching and shaking mops and brooms.

Irene, Dorothy, and a group of women: *(Holding their brooms and mops high, chanting)* Stand up for the strike! Clean up conditions in the mines! Stand up for the strike! Clean up conditions in the mines!

Stanley: Thomas, look at your mother and Dorothy and the other women. They're the ones who are going to be on the front page tomorrow.

Reporter: So, ladies, what's all this about?

Irene: We're marching for our husbands and sons. It's time to clean up the conditions in the mines. Their lives are at stake!

Dorothy: Tell your readers to support the miners. Tell the owners to listen to their demands. Even the President believes in our cause.

(The women march back and forth in front of the gates to the mine.)

Stanley: Well, Thomas, I think your mother and Dorothy are our own Mother Jones!

Thomas: *(Getting angry)* Pa, look, the soldiers are walking those workers over to the mine! Are they crossing the picket line?

(Some of the striking miners begin pushing the soldiers.)

Stanley: Thomas, hold your temper. The soldiers have guns. I don't want you to get shot. We've got to be careful or we'll lose more than our jobs.

Thomas: I know, Pa, but how can a miner refuse to strike? Look, there goes Mr. Simanski into the mine. How can he do that? He's just playing into the owners' hands and forgetting about his fellow miners.

Stanley: He has six children to feed at home, Thomas. He needs the pay. I know his heart is with us, but he has to do this for his family.

Thomas: But we are hurting, too, Pa. Dorothy had to take a job cleaning houses. She gets paid close to nothing for her hard work. There's a time when you have to take a stand.

(Some of the striking miners taunt the soldiers as they escort the workers to the mine. Others throw stones at the workers.)

Soldier: Get back, men. Let us through. Hey, back in line, or else.

Striking Miner: Or else what? You gonna shoot us? The reporters would love that. And it would make President Roosevelt mighty angry. He's on our side. He's meeting with our leaders now. Just you wait.

Soldier: Stay behind the lines! Let the workers pass!

Stanley: Get back, men. No need to give soldiers with guns a chance to shoot you.

Striking Miner: How can you do this? You take our jobs now, and when the strike is over, you'll be happy to take the wages we fought for. Well, just you wait! We'll remember your betrayal. You'll be out of work when we win our jobs back. We *all* voted to strike, and we'll remember who you are.

Reporter: So, Mr. Pilauski, you think that it's okay for some of the men to keep working?

Stanley: I think each man has to do what he thinks is right. He has to make his own choices. But sooner or later, a man has to have the courage to stand up for himself. As for me, I spend ten hours a day down where it's so dark, I need a lamp to see. My son does the same. We suffer so that *you* have coal to heat your home, to make factories run. I think that we deserve a fair shake.

Reporter: Can I quote you? That's not bad.

Stanley: You do your job, and I'll do mine.

(Peter appears, bringing lunch to his father and Thomas.)

Thomas: Peter, watch out, the strikers are throwing rocks at the soldiers. Get down, get down!

(A soldier fires his gun into the air.)

Stanley: Peter, this is getting too dangerous. I want you to get out of here right now. Go on, get home! Run as fast as you can and stay there.

Peter: But, Pa, I want to see the fights.

Thomas: Peter, do as Pa says. Get!

(Peter runs home just as another fight breaks out between the soldiers and the strikers.)

Scene 2

A miners' meeting at the gates of the mine

Narrator: President Roosevelt has forced the mine owners to work with the miners and settle their disputes in a process called **arbitration**. The miners are gathered at the gates of the mine to hear what has been decided. The miners are nervous and excited, hoping that they have won some of their demands.

Stanley: Calm down, men. Let's hear what happened with the President. We'll be able to gather our thoughts once we know what's going on.

---

arbitration – the act of having a person approved by both sides settle a dispute

Union Leader: Men, we have good news. The President met with the mine owners and us. He kept us there until we came to an agreement. Everybody had a chance to voice their views and come to an understanding of the situation.

Stanley: So, where does that leave us?

Thomas: Yeah, what about us? Do we go back to work? Do we get more money?

Union Leader: President Roosevelt set up a commission to settle the strike.

Striking Miner: A bunch of men who ain't never been in a mine? They'll side with the owners. I say we keep striking. We didn't stay out of work for months to be sold out now.

Stanley: Let's hear what happened. We don't know anything yet. Maybe we actually gained something.

Thomas: Yes, let's not make any hasty decisions.

Union Leader: Look, the commission is filled with men from both sides. We have representatives on it, too. President Roosevelt is a fair man. He didn't use the soldiers to break the strike. He made the owners sit down to talk. He wants to do what is best for all of us. What they are doing is called arbitration.

Thomas: What good is that?

Union Leader: It means both sides have to listen and the strike has to be settled. I have good news! We are going back to work! We will get paid more money, and we will get paid twice a month instead of once a month.

Miners: Hooray!

Stanley: Thomas, did you hear that? It looks like we're going back to the mines.

Thomas: Yeah, Pa. It does.

Stanley: When do we go back?

Union Leader: We return to work on Monday. We will strike until then.

Stanley: We'll have regular meals again. Come on, Thomas, let's get home and share the news.

Scene 3

In the streets outside the mine

Narrator: The strike is over. The union members are victorious. The miners will receive a wage increase of 10 percent and shorter workdays. They will work 9-hour days instead of 10- or 12-hour shifts. The miners take to the streets to celebrate. Thomas, however, has other things to think about. He has agreed to take a job working as a union organizer, so he will not be returning to the mines. But before he leaves the mines forever, he has a job to do.

Thomas: Well, Pa, I've been asked to work for the union. I'm going to have a job above ground.

Stanley: Well, come on, union man, that's good news. Let's go home and join the celebration in the streets.

Thomas: Okay, Pa, but first I've got something I have to do.

Stanley: What's that, son?

Thomas: Well, I need your help. Will you come with me? I've got to go down to the mine one more time.

Stanley: But Thomas, I thought you were done with the mine. Why on earth would you go down there again?

Thomas: You'll see. Just come down with me.

(They walk to a shed over a shaft of the mine.)

Elevator Man: I'll take ye down if ye need to go. Just step onto the platform over there. Not much going on in there today, though. Sort of strange, you wanting to go down there.

Thomas: Thanks, Willie. Yeah, we want to go down. Look at those dirty old cables, Pa. It's a wonder they haven't worn through by now. That's another thing the union can help change.

Elevator Man: Don't ye worry. They're good and strong. They can take ten men at a time easy.

Thomas: That's good, because I have a heavy load to bring up.

Stanley: What are you talking about, son? What are you going to do?

Thomas: I'm going to bring up Midnight, my mule. I'm going to get him out of this mine.

Stanley: You're what?

Thomas: Before the strike, the supervisor told me that Midnight was on his last legs. I don't know if he's still alive, since I haven't been down here in months. But if he is, he deserves a rest. I don't want Midnight to suffer the same fate as old Mr. Dugowitz. I don't want him to have to work until he dies.

Stanley: But, Thomas, they won't let you take the mule out. He belongs to the mine.

Thomas: No one will care if he's too old to work. I've got to see about him, Pa. I've spent every day of the last two years with him, and he's a good old mule. He's always been faithful and hardworking. I have to do it.

Stanley: Well, I guess I see what you mean.

(The wooden platform elevator reaches the bottom of the shaft and jolts to a stop on the ground. Thomas and Stanley get off.)

Thomas: Stay right here, if you will, Willie. We're going to bring my mule up.

Elevator man: Well, I don't usually bring the mules up this way, but I guess it don't matter. The elevator is plenty strong enough.

Thomas: Here he is, in his narrow little stall. Hey, whoa, boy. How are you doing? You don't look too good. Look how thin he is, Pa. He's not even standing with the other mules like he usually does.

Stable hand: Well, Thomas, I didn't expect to see anyone down here today. I just came down to feed the mules. Old Midnight's not strong enough to work any more. He still eats a little, and he's calm and steady. But I don't think he's going to last much longer.

Thomas: I've come down to take him out of the mine. I'm not going to be working in the mine anymore. So I thought I might take him up and let him have a chance to see the world one more time.

Stable hand: Well, you'll be doing him a favor, that's for sure. The supervisor said he wasn't earning his keep anymore. It's a good thing you came for him. I didn't want to think about burying him.

Thomas: Come on, Midnight, I'm taking you out of here. Here, Pa, help me get him onto the elevator.

Stanley: Do you think he'll get onto the elevator, Thomas?

Thomas: He's always done what I asked, Pa. He trusts me. He'll understand what I'm asking him to do.

Elevator man: Look at him, would ya? He's trembling. He knows he's going to see the sunshine again.

Thomas: He's going to see a pasture, too. I'm taking him to the barn where my friend mucks out the stalls. He'll be able to wander around and eat as much as he likes.

I'll visit him often, too. He's going to spend his last days breathing fresh air and feeling the sun on his back.

Stanley: You had this all planned out, didn't you, son?

Thomas: Yes, I've been thinking about it for a long time. I never thought I'd be able to do it. But Mother Jones was right. You have to keep on going even when the battle seems hopeless. And now Midnight and I are both going to have a new life.

Narrator: Stanley worked in the mines until he no longer could. At 45, he had to retire because his lungs were bad. They were filled with black dust. But Stanley was lucky. He didn't develop black lung disease. Slowly he recovered.

Thomas remained in Scranton and worked for the union. He became a union leader, married, and had a family. And he always remembered how happy he was the day he and Midnight left the mines forever.

Dorothy became a teacher. She married and moved to Philadelphia, where she taught school.

Peter never worked in the mines. He became a reporter for the paper. He wrote about abuses in the coal mines as well as in the meatpacking and auto industries. He took up the plight of the workers and told their stories.

Coal Mining in America

Coal Mines

In order to find coal, people create a coal mine. A coal mine is a series of tunnels and pits dug into the earth. Coal can be found close to the surface or hundreds of feet underground. The United States has a lot of coal. In fact, there is enough coal to supply the nation for many years. However, coal is a finite resource. This means once it is used, it cannot easily be replaced.

Modern coal miners use machines to dig for coal.

Coal mining in 1900

In the early 1900s, there were more than 700,000 coal miners in the United States. The job was hard and extremely dangerous. Coal miners worked in little or no light for up to 12 hours a day. The ceilings in the mines were low, and many miners had to work hunched over in tight spaces. Coal dust made it hard to breathe. Mines

The Uses of Coal in 1900 and Today		
1900	**Today**	**Use**
✓		To cook food
✓	✓	To run factories
✓		To power trains
	✓	To make medicine
	✓	To make plastics
✓	✓	To generate electricity
✓		To run home furnaces
✓	✓	To make steel
	✓	To be sold to other countries

were very hot in the summer and extremely cold in the winter. There was always the risk of a mine caving in or of an explosion in the mines. The miners were not paid well. They could be easily injured in an accident. Many miners also suffered from lung disease caused by breathing coal dust.

The 1902 Coal Miners' Strike

In 1902, coal miners in Pennsylvania decided to strike. They wanted better working conditions and more pay. On May 12, the coal miners' strike began. By October, people around the country were worried that there might not be enough coal for the winter. Finally, President Roosevelt stepped in and helped to settle the strike. The coal miners received a pay increase and shorter work days. The strike had been a success.

In the early 1900s, coal miners worked in very cramped spaces.

Write a Newspaper Article

Imagine the year is 1902. You are a reporter assigned to explain reasons for the coal miners' strike.

- Copy the chart shown below into your notebook.

- In the left column, list three events discussed in the story in the order they occurred.

- In the second column, list information about each event.

- Use the information from the story and other resources to complete your chart.

- Then write your article. Use dates and clue words such as *first, next, then,* and *last* to show the sequence of the events.

Events leading to strike	Information about the event
1. Mr. Dugowitz died in the mine.	• He was only 40 years old.
	• Many men are dying in the mines at a young age.
2.	
3.	

Read More About Workers' Rights

Find and read more books about workers' rights. As you read, think about these questions. They will help you understand more about this topic.

- Are there workers, in addition to coal miners, who had to fight for their rights in the 1900s?

- What are the risks and benefits of going on strike?

- Why is crossing a picket line such a serious decision?

- Why are certain employers against unions while their employees want to unionize?

SUGGESTED READING
Reading Expeditions
People Who Changed America: The Progressives

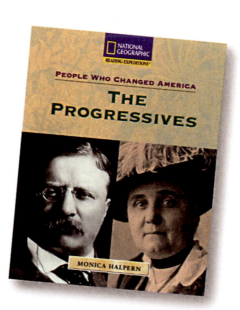